FATHER OF MANY NATIONS

FAITH-BUILDING STORIES

FOR KIDS

FATHER OF MANY NATIONS
FAITH-BUILDING STORIES
FOR KIDS

CARI HAUS

Autumn House® Publishing
www.autumnhousepublishing.com
A Division of **REVIEW AND HERALD® PUBLISHING**
Since 1861

Published by Autumn House® Publishing, a division of Review and Herald® Publishing, Hagerstown, MD 21741-1119

Autumn House® titles may be purchased in bulk for educational, business, fund-raising, or sales promotional use. For information, please e-mail SpecialMarkets@reviewandherald.com.

Autumn House® Publishing publishes biblically based materials for spiritual, physical, and mental growth and Christian discipleship.

The author assumes full responsibility for the accuracy of all facts and quotations as cited in this book.

Unless otherwise noted, texts are from the *Holy Bible, New International Version.* Copyright © 1973, 1978, 1984, International Bible Society. Used by permission of Zondervan Bible Publishers.

This book was
Edited by Penny Estes Wheeler
Cover design by Ron Pride
Cover art by Russ Harlan
Interior design by Candy Harvey
Electronic makeup by Shirley M. Bolivar
Typeset: 11/13 Cheltenham

PRINTED IN U.S.A.

11 10 09 08 07   5 4 3 2 1

Library of Congress Cataloging-in-Publication Data
Haus, Cari Hoyt.
 Father of many nations / Cari Haus.
     p. cm.
  ISBN 978-0-8127-0438-9
 1. Abraham (Biblical patriarch)—Juvenile literature.   I. Title.

BS580.A3H33 2007
 222'.1109505—dc22

                                        2006035709

Contents

CHAPTER 1

God Calls a Man

Throughout history it seems God has always had special jobs that needed to be done. It takes a special person to do God's special jobs—a friend of God who loves and understands his heavenly Father.

Soon after the Tower of Babel had tumbled, God was looking for such a person. No doubt if there had been help-wanted ads on the Internet during that time, God would have posted something like this:

"POSITION OPEN: Sincere person needed to stand up for God, living a holy life in a world filled with sin. Must be willing to teach his family and all who will listen about the one and only true God. Special bonus: the man chosen will be the father of many children. All families of the world will be blessed because of him. Must be willing to move as needed. No experience necessary. Will train."

Fortunately, God found just the man He needed for this special job. His name was Abram, a great-great-grandson of Shem. Abram must not have had to be perfect to be given the job, for the Bible tells us that his family worshipped idols as well as the true God. But somewhere along the line Abram chose to follow God, and God saw potential in him right from the start.

Abram was about 25 years old when God started unfolding a very exciting plan. We don't know just where Abram was when God called him. Perhaps he was by a burning bush like Moses, sleeping soundly like Samuel, or dreaming like the prophet Daniel. But we do know that Abram heard the voice of God one day, and that he listened to that voice—even above the hubbub of heathenism throbbing all around him.

"Abram, Abram," God called.

"Yes, Father?" No doubt Abram was surprised, since God had never spoken to him directly before.

"I have a special job for you to do."

"Yes, Father."

"I need a man to be the father of a great nation. I need a man who will keep the truth alive in the middle of heathen idol worshippers. I need one who will teach his children to love and honor Me and someday be the great-great-grandfather of My own Son when He comes to earth as a baby."

"Y-y-y-yes, Father!"

God called Abram to pick up where Adam, Abel, Seth, Enoch, Methusaleh, Noah, and Shem had left off. God called him to be the "keeper of the flame." He would be one in a line of holy men who would love and serve God, even in a world full of people who worshipped idols. Today these special torchbearers of the Bible are known as the patriarchs.

Because Abram said yes to God's call to serve Him in this way, God promised to give him a great blessing. In those days people really liked to have a *lot* of children, and Abram was no exception. He must have gotten pretty excited when God told him that he'd have so many children and grandchildren and great-great-great-great-great grandchildren that there'd be too many to count. God said that it would be like trying to count the grains of sand by the sea or the number of stars shining in the night.

Abram had a part to play as well. In order to be the Father of the Faithful, he must be faithful. He must be true to God, even when others weren't. God also asked Abram to move away from his family and friends. This was especially hard. People just didn't travel in those days as they do today. But God had a reason for asking Abram to move. He wanted him to stand out from the rest of the world, but He also knew that Abram's family could influence him to do wrong.

Abram's family worshipped the true God, but they had been slipping away from Him. While they still worshipped God in heaven, they also gave offerings to idols of wood, clay, and stone. Abram was in danger of becoming like them, so God asked him to move far away.

Abram could have quizzed God about where he was going, but he didn't. He could have asked God whether his new home would have sunshiny weather, rich soil, or money "growing on trees." But he didn't.

God had called Abram to follow Him, and Abram answered yes. It was as simple as that.

Today God stills calls people to help Him. Often He uses His still small voice, leading both kids and grown-ups through Bible study, prayer, and the things that happen in their lives. God calls some to leave places where they are wildly popular. Others are called to leave money, sports, fancy cars, families, friends, and other things that they love.

The path ahead often looks challenging. It may be filled with pain and sacrifice. But God has a special work for these special people. God knows it would be very hard for them to do these important things if they stayed close to the things they love most. So He calls them from people and places that might lead them into wrong, all the while drawing them closer and closer to His heart of love.

God still has His help-wanted ads posted today. He is looking for boys and girls and men and women who love Him so much that, if necessary, they will leave their hopes, dreams, and even their families to help Him finish His work. God needs people with firm and willing hearts who aren't afraid to go to new places or try new things if they can do it for Him.

Those who accept that call will have the faith of their father Abram. They will share with him that "far more exceeding and eternal weight of glory" that outweighs anything this aging world could ever hope to offer. Perhaps God is speaking to you today. Perhaps through this book He is asking you to love Him in a deeper, fuller way than you ever have before.

If so, there is only one question for you to answer: What will you do?

CHAPTER 2

Light in the Darkness

It's a wonderful fact of Scripture that those who choose to do God's will often bring at least some of their family and friends along with them. This is exactly what happened when Abram moved from Ur, the land of his childhood.

No doubt Abram's wife, Sarai, could have made his life miserable if she hadn't been willing to move. But we know she didn't, for the Bible speaks of how kind and thoughtful she was to her husband. And what a job she must have had—packing for such a strange trip! You can imagine the neighbor ladies dropping in on Sarai, and what their conversations might have been like.

"Where did you say you were moving, Sarai?"

"H'mmm . . . I guess I really don't know."

"How long do you think it will take you to get to—wherever?"

"I'm afraid I don't know that either."

"If you don't know where you are going or when you will get there, why in the world do you want to move?"

"It's not a matter of what we do or don't want. We're just doing what God asked Abram to do."

No doubt Abram discussed his plans with the men of Ur as he worked in the fields or took his grain to market. Some of them caught a vision of God through the lives and excitement of Abram and Sarai and joined them on their journey of faith.

One of those joining up for the trip was Terah, Abram's father. Abram's nephew, Lot, also decided to go along.

Abram had a great number of servants, and they were going too. And then friends of Abram's family joined the trip. These friends had come to love and know the true God through the loving, godly lives of Abram and Sarai. They wanted to worship the true God and be with others who loved Him, even if it meant leaving their families far behind.

When you add all these family, friends, and servants to the great number of camels, donkeys, and sheep that Abram already had, it was quite a caravan leaving Ur of the Chaldees. No doubt the *Chaldees Chronicle,* if there was such a thing, ran a front-page story about the whole operation. "Wealthy Caravan Moving to Who Knows Where" could have been the headline.

The first big stop for the large caravan was in

Haran, where they lived until after the death of Terah, Abram's father. Perhaps Terah was an old man when they started the journey, and in His mercy God allowed the caravan to rest while the grandfather of the faithful lived out his final days. Whatever the reason, Abram waited patiently in Haran until the voice of God once again whispered in his ear, telling him to move on.

The town of Shechem was the next stop on Abram's long journey. It was a beautiful place. There were grassy valleys watered by rushing springs and fields of wheat and barley. The land was rich with fig and olive trees, olive oil, and honey.

Unfortunately, there was also a curse in the vale of Shechem, for "the Canaanite was then in the land." On the wooded hilltops stood altars—not to the God of heaven, but to the many false gods of the Canaanites. Surely Abram and Sarai were horrified to learn that children were sacrificed on these altars. And the other heathen habits of these godless people must have made them sick.

As might be imagined, the unkindness and cruelty going on all around him made Abram very uneasy. He clung to promises God had given him. But the more he knew about his violent heathen neighbors, the more fear filled his heart. Just when Abram was really starting to get worried—in his hour of greatest need—he once again felt a heavenly hand on his shoulder.

The Bible says, "But the Lord appeared to Abram, and said, 'To your offspring I will give this land'" (Genesis 12:7). Abram was worried about whether he could even survive during those terrible days, but

God let him know that not only would he survive, he would live happily and prosper. This land would even be given to his children and grandchildren. God also told Abram that He would be with him and protect him from the dangers about him.

Encouraged by God's promise, Abram built an altar where he'd met God. What a refreshing change Abram's altar must have been from the hundreds of altars dotting the Canaanite hillsides. Here, right in the middle of a heathen culture, stood an altar to the living God. And it was here in the darkness of heathenism that God wanted Abram's light to shine.

From that time on, it seemed that Abram was always building altars. In fact, he gathered stones and built an altar wherever he pitched his tent. There at those family altars Abram held regular family worship for anyone who wanted to come. As Adam, Abel, Methusaleh, Noah, and so many others had done before him, Abram offered an innocent lamb on the altar and told others what God had done for him, how He forgave sin. No doubt they sang songs around the altar as well, as the heavenly angelic choir looked approvingly down from heaven.

When it was time for Abram to move on, he always left his altar behind. Those altars became a witness to the Canaanites. Many knew about the God of heaven because of Abram and Sarai. Later, when the roving Canaanites stumbled upon one of Abram's altars, they always knew who had been there before them.

"This is Abram's altar," they told their children, "the altar of the living God." Then sometimes they repaired the altar and together with their families worshipped God themselves. And so the godly influence and example of Abram spread in the land of Canaan as others learned of the true God through his humble, traveling servant.

CHAPTER 3

A Trouble-filled Trip

It would be nice if Abram, after leaving so much behind in Ur to follow God's leading, lived happily ever after. But that's not the way it was. You see, God in His great mercy often uses the trials and trouble of life to make us strong. And God was working with Abram, leading him to trust in his heavenly Father more and more every day.

It seems that the land of Canaan, which had been so beautiful when Abram first arrived, went without rain for quite some time. The bubbling brooks dried up, and the grassy green fields turned to a withered-up brown. Abram's servants scrambled to find pasture and water for the many animals their master owned. As things got worse they started to wonder whether they could find enough water and food for their own families.

"I wonder what Abram is thinking now," whispered one herdsman to another. "Do you think he wishes he were back in our old home in the well-watered meadows of the Chaldean plains?"

As Abram's troubles piled up, every eye in the camp was on him. Eagerly his family, friends, and servants watched and waited to see what he would do. He was their leader, and, as long as he seemed sure that things would work out well, the people were confident too.

"God is Abram's friend," they said to one another. "As long as God is still guiding Abram, everything will be OK."

Abram had no idea why there was a drought in the land with little water or grass for their flocks. This certainly was not what he'd hoped for. Yet he trusted God to make it all right in the end.

"I will bless you and make your name great," God had promised. Clinging to that promise, Abram spent more time than ever in prayer. Again and again he asked his heavenly Father what he should do to save the lives of his family, friends, and servants from the dreadful fate of starvation.

Abram knew God had called him to Canaan. But there was no food in Canaan, so he decided to move to Egypt. He would stay as close as he could to the Promised Land until God should lead him back.

Abram didn't know it then, but God had allowed this trouble for a reason. God was teaching Abram important lessons of obedience, patience, and faith.

These lessons would not only make Abram fit to be the father of the faithful, they would be an example for all God's children who ran into trouble in their lives.

God sometimes leads His children in ways they don't understand. Sometimes we pass through dark valleys, but God never forgets or forsakes us. He is like a loving shepherd. We should be His trusting sheep.

In Bible times so many bad things happened to a man named Job that even today people say they "feel like Job" when many, many things go wrong. But through all of Job's troubles God never left his side. Then there was the disciple John. He could have felt forsaken and forgotten when he was exiled on the lonely island of Patmos. Just when it seemed all hope was lost, God appeared to John. There on the rocky shores heaven came down and touched this earth in visions and scenes of glory.

Today God still allows troubles and trials to bother His faithful servants. God knows that if you are steadfast, faithful, and obedient even when things go bad, you will become rich in a spiritual way. And as you weather the storms and trials of life, you can become a source of help and strength to others.

God doesn't like to see anyone suffer. Yet He knows that the problems and trials that make our lives hard, and that may even make us wonder whether God has forgotten us, will actually lead us closer to Him. God wants us to lay all our troubles down at His feet. Only then can He give us the peace that is so wonderful we can't even understand it.

"'For I know the plans I have for you,' declares the Lord, 'plans to prosper you and not to harm you'" (Jeremiah 29:11).

When a goldsmith refines precious metal, he uses a very hot furnace to separate the true gold from everything else. God is like a goldsmith. Sometimes He lets His children suffer in the furnace of problems to bring out the glimmering gold of a godly Christian character.

Just like a goldsmith, God carefully watches the "fire." He is the master craftsman. He knows how hot is too hot, and He also knows how hot it must be before the golden characters burnished in the fire will reflect the radiance of His love.

God sees the talents and helpful character traits in each of His children. He knows the talents you have, and how they may be used in His work of saving others. So He lets trouble into your life, not to make you unhappy, but to help you turn to Him and trust Him to shelter you under His wings.

When you go through unhappy times, you will learn things about yourself that you never knew before. You may see your own faults more clearly. Perhaps you notice that you are short-tempered, or other weaknesses will stand out.

When this happens, God is giving you chances to change your character. He wants you to be fitted up for His service. God also wants you to learn to lean on Him and to know that He is your only help and safety.

As you learn to trust God more, you will reach His great purpose for your life. You will be educated, trained, and disciplined, ready to fulfill the grand plan that God has for you. Then when He calls you to spring into action, you'll be ready! Like Adam and Abel, Enoch and Noah, Abram, and so many others, you'll be working with God and the angels to do the very important task of helping others get ready for heaven.

The Tainted (Un)Truth

Every now and then a person or place or thing stands out above all the rest. Sometimes it's the tallest teenager who catches your eye, or the cutest puppy, or the buck with the biggest antlers.

We already know that Abram was a very rich man, for the Bible tells us so. But the Bible also has some things to say about Abram's wife. She was a beautiful woman—so strikingly pretty that it would be hard for anyone not to notice.

There was just something about her. Perhaps it was a combination of inner and outer beauty that made Sarai stand out above all the rest. Whatever it was,

Abram knew that he was married to an incredibly gorgeous woman. In fact, everyone who came within squinting distance of his camp knew it. That is, of course, exactly what worried Abram as he packed up his camp to go to the land of Egypt because of the famine in Canaan.

You see, those were pretty tough times back then. They were like the world was before the Flood and the way it is in some places today. Although Abram loved God and honored Him by his godly life, there were plenty of people who didn't. They didn't obey God's rules, and if they saw their neighbor with something (or somebody!) they wanted, they didn't mind killing or stealing to have their way.

When the Egyptians see Sarai, Abram thought in his heart, *someone will want her for his wife.* Since the Egyptians didn't serve the God of heaven, Abram knew what would most likely happen next.

They'll just come and take her, he thought. *And if they know I am her husband, they'll kill me first.*

This was quite a lapse of faith for the future father of the faithful, but it shows just how human Abram was. He loved Sarai. In fact, they had grown up together. But he didn't want to die. And since he wasn't sure how God would work all this out, he took matters into his own hands.

In those days people had huge families, and men sometimes married a cousin or even a half-sister. That is how it came about that in addition to being Abram's wife, Sarai was also his half-sister. Whether Abram's mother had died before Sarai was born, we don't know. But we do know that Terah was the father of both Abram and Sarai, and that they had dif-

ferent mothers. That is exactly what Abram was thinking when he asked Sarai to tell a half-truth.

"Why don't we tell the Egyptians that you are my sister?" Abram asked his wife. He was hoping that she wouldn't be noticed, but if she was, he wanted a plan.

It turned out that Abram was right about the Egyptians noticing Sarai. The Egyptian men took note of her right away. And word traveled fast, for it didn't take long before a description of Sarai reached the interested ears of Pharaoh.

Of course, Pharaoh probably already had a wife. In fact, he may well have had 20. But the point is, he thought he might need another.

"Send and get her," he ordered his royal courier. So it wasn't long before Pharaoh's servants arrived at Abram's camp. No doubt Abram gave Sarai a look when he saw them coming, as she quickly ducked into a tent.

"The king would like to ask about one of the women who lives in your camp," the Egyptian told Abram.

"And may I ask which one?"

I'm sure Abram hoped the king might have his eye on some single young maiden rather than his own dear Sarai.

"Her name is Sarai." The Egyptian studied Abram closely. "Is she any relation to you?"

Abram tried to still his pounding heart. "She is my sister," he murmured. Of course, what he said was true. But it was only half true, and God expects more from His people.

Since Sarai was "only" Abram's sister and the king wanted her very badly, the Egyptians insisted on taking her with them right then. Perhaps they thought she would be glad to come with them. Living in the king's palace, she would have many good things. But it was a sad goodbye for Abram and Sarai. They had no idea how or whether they would ever meet again.

Fortunately, our God in heaven oversees everything that happens to us. He was watching Abram and Sarai at this unhappy moment, and as He has done so many times in this world's history, He stepped in to save His children from themselves.

God already had a plan for Abram and Sarai's lives. The fact that God had promised to make Abram the father of many nations could mean only one thing for Sarai. She would be the mother of many nations. Of course, none of this could happen if Sarai became queen of Egypt or even just one of the king's pretty wives. And so in His great mercy God sent Pharaoh a special and very personal message.

The Bible doesn't go into a lot of detail, but we do know that God sent some trouble into the houses of Pharaoh and his servants. It was the kind of trouble that could be undone, for God understood the Egyptian king's heart. While the king was heathen and worshipped many idols, he had a good sense of right and wrong. Though others might have stolen another man's wife, this king would not have done so—at least, not if he'd known the truth.

"What is this you have done to me?" Pharaoh thundered to Abram after the truth came out. "Why did you say she was your sister when in fact she was your wife?"

Pharaoh had a right to be angry. He had treated Abram very well, but his kindness had been rewarded with an embarrassing lie.

"Here is your wife." Pharaoh pointed toward the door. "Take her, and get out of my country."

Pharaoh had good reason for sending Abram out of the country. He had seen how God blessed and protected Abram, even when the man did wrong, and he was afraid to have them stay in Egypt.

"What if one of my people hurts this man?" Pharaoh asked his advisers. "Then his God will hold me responsible and punish my kingdom." So Pharaoh sent another messenger, whose job it was to escort Abram safely out of his country.

In the years that followed, the experience of Abram in Egypt helped protect him from the wicked and often violent people who lived all around his camp. They knew Abram was under God's special protection. Because of this, those who might otherwise have tried to hurt him were afraid to do so. As the king of Egypt so quickly learned, it is a dangerous thing to hurt a child of the King of heaven—even when that child has done something wrong.

In the book of Psalms, David writes that God "reproved kings" for the sake of His children. In addition, the ungodly are warned: "Do not touch my anointed ones, and do my prophets no harm" (Psalm 105:14, 15).

In many ways Abram's experience in Egypt was like that of his children's children many years later. Like Israel, Abram went into Egypt to escape from a famine. Like his future offspring, Abram was protected by God. As a result of that protection of both Abram and the children of Israel, the fear of God fell on the Egyptian nation. That is why the Egyptians gave both Abram and his descendants many gifts, and they left the land of Egypt with a lot of things and money.

CHAPTER 5

Cities of the Plain

What are you doing here?"

Abram's head herdsman jammed his shepherd's rod into the dew-covered grass and planted a swarthy hand on his hip.

"What are *you* doing here?" Lot's herdsman shot back, digging his giant sandals into the grass.

"I'll tell you exactly why we're here," thundered Abram's servant. "This is the only meadow left that your monstrous herds haven't devoured. All I want is grass, but everywhere I go, guess who's there? Lot's men, Lot's sheep, and Lot's camels. Why, I don't believe there's a sprig of grass left in this whole voluminous valley your goats haven't gobbled into stubble. And I'm here to tell you something: this is *my* meadow. I got here first, and I aim to feed my flock right here, right now. So move your herds along, buddy."

Abram's servant glared at his challenger, but the man didn't flinch.

"Don't waste your long speeches on me," he bellowed, reaching for his sword. "I've got a job to do here. Get your huge herd of heifers out of my way."

"I won't!" shouted Abram's man.

"You will!" shouted Lot's, moving his face so close that the two could smell each other's breath.

"Just a minute, you two!" The angry herdsmen postponed their punching match at the sound of an all-too-familiar voice. It was Abram, out with Lot to check on the cattle.

"Oh, excuse me, master." Abram's servant whirled around in shocked embarrassment. "I didn't know you were here."

"I understand we have a shortage of pastureland," Abram sighed as he turned to his nephew. He was fond of Lot and didn't want him to move away. But this continual bickering between the herdsmen got worse all the time.

The two angry men opened their mouths to launch into their sides of the story but stopped short when Abram held up his hand.

"Just a minute, gentlemen."

Lot's herdsman nodded politely to Abram, then cast a last glare at his rival before backing away. "You won't need to discuss this anymore. Lot and I will work something out."

The younger man nodded politely, then turned to

follow Abram down a well-traveled path. Passing through the overgrazed meadow, they started up the highest nearby hill and at last stood at the summit. Below them stretched vast valleys of closely nibbled grass, and beyond that fields of green that seemed to stretch all the way to the sky.

For a while the two men stood silently, comparing the distant green beauty with the nubby brown fields just below them. At last Abram spoke.

"This is truly hard for me, son." He looked fondly at his nephew. "God has blessed us so greatly that I fear there are no pastures large enough for us to share the same camp."

"Yes, Uncle." Lot shifted from one foot to another, wondering what his uncle would suggest. As the younger of the two, he looked up to his uncle Abram. After the death of Lot's father, it was Abram who had taken the young man under his wing. He had taught him how to care for the animals, how to be a successful businessman, and how to know the true God.

Abram was a strong and wise man. Even the heathen who lived all around them looked up to him. And because of everything Abram had done for him and all that he meant to him, Lot probably thought of Abram as more of a father than an uncle. In those days even grown men treated their fathers with great respect. The oldest grandpa in a family was called the patriarch, and even his grown sons obeyed him.

Lot should have been thinking about all these things during this most critical moment of his life. But he wasn't. Instead, his mind raced forward as his eyes roved over the lush green hills gleaming in the distance.

"I feel we must separate, Lot." Abram's kind and courteous voice broke into the younger man's thoughts.

"Which part of the valley would you like, Uncle?" In his heart Lot knew that Abram should have first choice. After all, God had given the entire country to his uncle.

Abram spread one arm toward the east and one toward the west, making a human compass with his body.

"You decide, Lot," he said in his usual gracious, courteous way.

Lot stared at his uncle in shocked amazement. Could it really be true? Was Uncle Abram really letting him, the younger and less established of the two, have first pick of the property spread out below them? If so, this was the financial opportunity of a lifetime. There was money to be made in those hills. You see, nestled in the valleys, surrounded by the rich green grass and bubbling springs so beautiful that the land was compared to the Garden of Eden, were the thriving cities of Sodom and Gomorrah.

Lot knew about these cities of the plain, and so did Abram. Both men had been there, stayed there, and done business with the men of those cities. Abram and Lot were also both well aware of one very clear fact: though the cities were very rich, they were also very wicked. In fact, they were so wicked they had actually become famous for being so evil.

In all his travels Abram had always taken care to protect his family from the wicked world surrounding them. Knowing that he had been called to leave his family to better serve God, Abram had tried to protect those in his camp from the terrible sins committed by many of their neighbors. As a man who believed in God, Lot should have been careful too. But somehow, in that all-important moment of decision, all Lot could think about was green. The money was not green back then, but the grass surely was. And it translated into easy living and wealth in Sodom and Gomorrah, the cities of the plains.

Lot nodded courteously to his uncle.

"Thank you for your generosity," he said. Then he spread his arms as if to encircle the cities, the wicked but beautiful cities of the plain.

"I will take the land over here," Lot said. Like so many people today, Lot made the awful mistake of putting money before spiritual things. And so, in one selfish moment, an otherwise good man chose to move his family next to some very evil influences. The Bible says that he pitched his tent toward Sodom and Gomorrah.

CHAPTER 6

Battle of the Kings

There must have been a lot of sad goodbyes the day Lot moved away from Abram. Abram and Sarai wouldn't see him or his family anymore, for people didn't travel then as we do today. Sarai may have been close to Lot's little daughters, especially since she had no children of her own.

Then there were Lot's herdsmen, his servants, and all of their families. They too had learned to love God through the example set by Abram and Sarai. In spite of their not having enough pasture for the flocks of both men, many of them must have had close friends in the encampment where Abram and his people lived.

But the day came when the last donkey was saddled, the last camel packed, and the last tearful goodbye said. Lot and his family were off to start life near the cities, while Abram and Sarai settled back into their own lives. And they led quite a life, for by this time Abram was a very rich man. His camp of more than a thousand people must have buzzed like a small town on a very busy day. There was always something going on. While many of these people were Abram's servants, others simply wanted to live near people who loved and honored the true God.

Abram and his camp lived in a land of idol worship. Some people even sacrificed their children to idols. But Abram's life shone like a bright light for the God he loved. Their heathen neighbors had abandoned God, and crime and wickedness filled their lives. This made Abram's beautiful character stand out even more, for he was a kind, noble, and truly unselfish man.

Abram and Sarai took good care of the many members of their large household, too. And by their kind example many others came to know and love God.

The heathen people living all around recognized that Abram was a good man and looked up to him. They also knew he was no pushover, for he had 318 servant-soldiers as part of his camp. Abram didn't like to fight, and he never wanted to kill. But in those very difficult days, leaders such as Abram had to defend their people. And so they did.

One day Abram received a message from some of the kings in the area. Any time they had to go to battle they wanted Abram on their side. By joining together they were better able to fight off invading armies.

Unfortunately, one army had already invaded their land. Chedorlaomer, king of Elam, had conquered the country 14 years earlier, and everyone had to pay taxes to him. The conquered kings didn't like this, so they banded together to fight for the rights of their kingdoms.

King Chedorlaomer wouldn't stand for this uprising, so he recruited four other rulers to help put down the rebellion. It was a battle of 10 kings—five against five, and it couldn't have gone much worse for the kings of Canaan. War is always terrible, and this war was no different. After defeating the kings of Canaan, King Chedorlaomer and his friends plundered the cities of the plains, killing, stealing, and taking captives.

The captives were forced to march the long way back to the main camp of their enemies. Camels, sheep, and cattle had been captured too and were driven along behind the people. In addition to people and animals, the armies had plundered gold and silver and other precious things from the people they'd conquered. The kings were ready for a party, for they had plenty to celebrate.

Sodom and Gomorrah were two of the cities raided—the modern cities where Lot had taken his family to live. What a shock it must have been to be captured as common criminals. Lot had moved to Sodom to make his fortune, but things were very bad now.

While the victors celebrated with alcohol and shrieks of joy, the horror and sadness of the captives must have been just as intense. How Lot longed for the streets of Sodom, where he'd lived so safely just a few hours before. Compared to being captured and imprisoned by his enemies, even the peaceful fields he'd left to his uncle Abram must have looked pretty good. Of course, that was where Abram was at that very moment—living peacefully in the plain of Mamre. No doubt he was taking care of some routine matter when he saw a runner on a distant hill. The man was alone, running desperately from the horrible scenes behind him.

Abram watched as the runner got nearer and nearer, huffing and puffing for air with each step.

"The cities of the plain have been overthrown!" he gasped as Abram ran out to meet him. "Sodom and Gomorrah were raided, and many have been taken captive!"

Now it was Abram's turn to gasp in shock and surprise.

"What about my nephew Lot?" were the first words out of his lips.

Quickly Abram called his men together, for he was a man of action. He didn't like to fight, but he would fight for Lot and his family.

What a prayer meeting they must have had at Abram's altar just before he left. There was danger ahead, and they knew it.

"It is well worth the risk," Abram must have told Sarai as he kissed her goodbye. "I'll soon be back, and by God's grace Lot and his family will be with me."

Abram's strategy was simple. He would catch the invaders by surprise and uproot them while they were still lolling around, hungover from the alcohol they'd drunk at a huge party the night before.

We don't know what time of the day Abram and

his men left, but they must have ridden hard to catch King Chedorlaomer. Perhaps they rode all night and all the next day, arriving near the enemy camp late the next night.

There the tied-up captives sat, alert and sleepless, as enemy soldiers snored nearby. Then a shout was heard from the hilltop.

"Attack!"

"W-w-w-what?" A groggy Elamite soldier covered his aching head with his arms. "I must be having a bad dream."

And he was having a bad "dream"—only this time the nightmare was real. Of course, it was a dream come true for the captives. The torches held by Abram's men shone from every hilltop as their shouts rang into the valley. Somehow in the darkness and confusion that small band of soldiers made enough noise to sound like 3,000 men. In the torchlight the captives from Sodom saw the terrible scenes of battle, heard the cries of the wounded, and watched as mighty King Chedorlaomer himself lost his life.

How they must have huddled together to keep clear of the swinging swords as Abram and his fighting men vanquished the enemy army. How tears of joy must have streamed down their faces as the morning light dawned and they were captives no more. Many hands cut or untied their bonds. They were free! Free to go home to their beautiful cities once again.

"Uncle Abram!"

We can only imagine Lot's joy to see his long-lost uncle, especially at the unhappiest moment of his life.

Then it was Abram's turn to have a party—and it

must have been a strange one at that. For though he was celebrating with the kings of Canaan—men who loved to drink and dance the whole night through—Abram had an entirely different type of celebration.

"Praise God!"

I can hear him singing. It would have been just like him to build an altar right then and there, offering a lamb to the God he loved so much. Perhaps God even *whooshed* fire out of heaven in front of the king of Sodom, letting all who saw it know that Abram really was His man.

Though we don't know the details, we can be sure there was a whole lot of singing and rejoicing in Abram's camp when he and his men returned home. Perhaps Sarai, like her great-great-granddaughter Miriam, was a great singer. Maybe she led the women in a great and special song of thanksgiving to God. If so, we can be sure that the angels of heaven were leaning out of the gates once more, hitting notes higher than all of the rest. And the hearts of the heathen were strangely warmed as they saw religion in action, a God-centered party, and the unselfish example of the noble man who had fought to save them all.

No doubt God tugged at their heartstrings—giving them a glimpse of the peace they could have if they would only turn to Him. For God loved the people of Sodom and Gomorrah. He had even loved King Chedorlaomer. And He wanted those who had survived the horrible scenes of war to turn their hearts to Him before it became too late.

CHAPTER 7

Old Testament Shell Shock

Once the war was over Abram had some very trouble-some thoughts. He had always been a man of peace. He wasn't used to killing and bloodshed and pain. He was also troubled by the idea that the nations he conquered would again grow strong and come back to take revenge.

There was a lot of fighting in those days. A lot of ar-guments were settled with the sword. Abram had been living in peace, hating the very idea of war. There was only one reason he had even gotten in-volved—to save his nephew Lot.

Now, however, Abram found himself really worried about the future. Then God, who was watch-ing over Abram all the time and knew about his worries, had a word with his faithful servant.

"Don't worry, Abram," a voice boomed out in the night. Abram had been tossing and turning in his tent when God spoke to him in a dream. "I will take care of you, shield you from danger, and be very good to you." God also repeated His promise that Abram would be the father of many nations.

"Could you please give me a sign so that I'll know this is true?" Abram asked God. He was having trouble wrapping his mind around all that God had just said. He and Sarai were getting very old, and they still had no children. How could God still say that he, Abram, would be the father of many nations?

Now Abram had an idea. "What about my good servant Eliezer?" he asked. "I could adopt him and have children that way."

In answer to Abram's question God led him outside to look at the stars. Abram looked up and saw thousands and thousands of stars shining against the black sky. No smog or city lights hid them from view.

"Do you see all those stars?" God asked Abram.

"Yes, Lord."

"Can you count them?"

"No, Lord."

"That's how many children you will have, and they will be your very own children, *not* Eliezer's."

As Abram looked up into the sky it suddenly seemed possible that he, an old man without children, could still be the father of a large nation. The Bible tells us that he "believed God, and it was counted unto him for righteousness" (Romans 4:3; see Genesis 15:6). Yet still he begged for a sign.

So God did something very important for Abram. He had him prepare some animal sacrifices and had a very special ceremony to show that He was making a covenant—or a promise—with Abram that would never be broken.

All day long Abram watched over the sacrifices so that birds and other animals couldn't bother them. In the evening, feeling very tired, he fell fast asleep. Soon it became dark—so dark you could feel it. Abram opened his eyes and saw a blazing torch moving among the sacrifices. God Himself had come down to earth and was burning them up.

"I will give you this land. I promise," God told Abram. God told Abram a lot of very important things that night. He told him that even though the land of Canaan would belong to his children, it wouldn't happen right away. God explained that Abram's children would go through some hard times first.

Abram woke up from his dream feeling very encouraged. His fear went away, because he knew that even though his life would not always be easy, God would be there for him.

The years passed. Life was busy and life was good except that Abram and Sarai still had not had the child God had promised.

Then again God came to Abram to remind him of the promise He had made. "Even though she is old," God said, "Sarai will be the mother of the child you will have."

Then God did something even more special. He gave both Abram and Sarai new names. Abram would be called Abraham, which means "father of a great multitude." And Sarai would be Sarah, because, God said, "she shall be a mother of nations, kings shall be of her."

God also gave Abram some rules for his people to live by. He reminded Abram that his children should not marry people who didn't love the true God of heaven. He also talked to Abram about how his children would be different from the people all around them. And God reminded Abram that his life would not always be easy.

It might have been hard for Abraham the very next morning when he told his servants about his new name.

"Father of a multitude," some of the sarcastic ones must have snickered. "Why, he's old enough to be a great-grandfather, and he doesn't have even one baby!"

But that didn't stop Abraham from going by his new name. And every time someone called it, Abraham was reminded of God's promise. He might not have any children yet, but he was going to. God had said it, Abraham believed it, and that settled it for him.

CHAPTER 8

Angels at Noonday

With all the servants, camels, sheep, and other animals Abraham owned, he must have been a very busy man. Just imagine—we read earlier that Abraham had 318 soldiers. These were men who were young and strong enough to serve as soldiers in his camp. If he had more than 300 soldiers, he probably had quite a few more men who were too old to join the fight. If most of those men had wives, and many of them had children and even grandchildren, Abraham could easily have had a few thousand people working for or living very close to him.

Sometimes when people get too busy or too important, they don't take time for others. But that wasn't the case with Abraham. He had a special gift that we should all want—the gift of hospitality.

People with the gift of hospitality are good at making others feel comfortable and welcome. Real experts at this can hide their shock and surprise when people show up uninvited, even if they got the wrong address and think you invited them over for dinner!

Of course, to be that good at hospitality you have to plan for it. You can help keep your house neat and clean so you can happily welcome anyone at just about any time.

It's important to be flexible enough that you can drop everything for a bit and make even uninvited quests feel welcome. This is especially hard in today's busy world. But we should ask God to help us have the heavenly gift of hospitality.

Even if things aren't just right in your home, there are many ways to be friendly. If your cupboard is empty, try keeping lemonade on hand to serve. If your house is a mess, you can visit with folks on the porch.

Abraham liked to keep an eye down the road to see whether people were coming. Then he would run out to meet them and invite them to stay and eat with him. Sarah and the servants would fix a great meal; then Abraham and his guests would enjoy eating and visiting.

Of course, in those long-ago times there were no radios or TVs, so meeting people from afar was a great way to hear the news and get new ideas. There were always political happenings and the weather to talk about. Maybe they even discussed the best ways to raise camels or survive a desert sandstorm.

In any case, one day as Abraham rested in the doorway of his tent he saw three strangers walking down the road. Just as he always did, Abraham hurried to invite them to stop and eat with him. He also sent a message to Sarah to start making a special meal.

Abraham was so courteous that he didn't even eat while his guests were eating. Though he was one of the richest men in the world, he stood by as a host to total strangers, making sure they had plenty to eat and anything else they might need.

When Abraham invited the men in for dinner he had no idea who they were. He treated them just the same as he would have treated anyone else who came down the road. But God had a very special treat in store for Abraham that day. Because Abraham had honored God, God chose to honor him by coming to earth with two angels to walk and talk with him. They had something important to tell him.

"Shall I hide the thing I am about to do from Abraham?" God turned and spoke to one of the angels. "I have heard that Sodom and Gomorrah are very wicked, so I came down to take a look so that I would know for Myself."

Of course, He knew very well exactly what was going on in Sodom and Gomorrah. God is everywhere and knows everything, so He didn't need to come down. But this is the kind of God we serve. He is fair, He is love, and He checks things out for Himself.

You may have heard of a very important sounding phrase: the investigative judgment. It sounds

hard to understand, but to *investigate* just means to check something out or look into it.

Some people find it hard to believe that an investigative judgment is going on right now in heaven. But there were plenty of investigative judgments in the Bible. Before God punished Adam and Eve for their sin in the Garden of Eden, He Himself came down and talked to them. Before God destroyed the Tower of Babel, He came down to see for Himself what was going on. And before He got serious about punishing Sodom and Gomorrah, He once again came down to take a look. That is the kind of God we serve. Although He loves us very much, at some point He will punish the wicked. But He doesn't go just by hearsay.

When Abraham realized that he was standing near the living God, he was overcome with reverence and humility. He understood how great God really is, and how we should act in His presence. But while Abraham was reverent, he was also bold. When Sodom and Gomorrah were mentioned, Abraham's first thought was of his dear nephew Lot. He didn't want Lot or his family to be hurt.

"O Lord," begged Abraham, shifting his feet, "please do not be angry with me, for I am being very bold." Abraham did not try to impress God with his riches or remind Him that he had been obedient or made many sacrifices. Instead, he was like a confident child pleading with his father.

"I know You are fair and loving," Abraham said. "I know You wouldn't even think of punishing the innocent, good people with the bad. That would be far from You, Lord."

God didn't say anything yet, but Abraham knew He was listening.

"Would You destroy the city if there were 50 good people living there?"

"No, I would save it for 50 good people," God replied.

Abraham felt much better—for about five seconds. Then he thought about how wicked those cities were, and wondered whether there were even 50 good people there. So he asked God the same question again and again, each time going lower and lower on his number.

Abraham was very polite and respectful about the whole thing, and God didn't seem to mind that he kept asking. And so the number went from 50 to 45 to 40, then 30, 20, and 10—and the answer was always the same. "If there were that many good people there, I would not destroy the city."

Abraham's care and concern for Sodom and Gomorrah is an example for us today. Like God, Abraham hated sin, but he loved sinners. He did not want to see anyone lost. He was very determined in going back to God over and over again to see whether the whole city could be saved for just a few good folks.

At last Abraham felt satisfied. "There must be at least 10 good people in Lot's family alone," he murmured to himself as he said goodbye to God and the two angels that were with Him. Then Abraham went back to his tent to watch and wait, and the heavenly travelers went to visit the city—the beautiful but very wicked city of Sodom.

CHAPTER 9

Sodom's Last Sunset

If you've ever watched the Olympics, you probably know that this grand series of athletic races always takes place in one of the world's finest cities. In fact, there is even a contest of sorts to decide which city is the best and most beautiful place to host the Olympic Games.

There were no Olympics in Abraham's day—at least, not that we know of. But if there had been, the city of Sodom would most likely have won it. Without a doubt, Sodom had the most mouth-watering food, the most impressive buildings, and the most gorgeous gardenlike parks a person could hope for in even a dream vacation. For like the Bahamas or Hawaii or the

Galapagos Islands, Sodom was truly a tropical paradise.

Towering palm trees shaded the busy streets, while the perfume of a thousand flowers wafted into the air. Because the weather was always right, food grew fast and there was plenty for all. Business boomed inside the city gates. Sodom was the entertainment capital of the Canaanite plains, the Sodomite stock exchange was at an all-time high, and it seemed that money almost sprouted on trees.

Camel caravans from the East constantly arrived with precious stones and perfumes and artwork for the markets of Sodom. And as kind of an artsy tourist town, Sodom was filled with craftsmen, painters, and potters. These artists liked to outdo one another, painting and sculpting and weaving the finest artwork that money could buy. There probably weren't any slums in Sodom, either—only streets with names like Wealthy Street, Prosperity Parkway, and Bankers Boulevard.

But unfortunately, there were some very bad things about Sodom. Because the people were so rich and had so much spare time on their hands, they loved luxurious living. Worse than that, their wealth had made them haughty and proud. They didn't know what it was like to be poor, sad, or even very busy, so their hearts became hard and cruel. God had blessed them with lots of free time and money, but they used these blessings only for themselves. They became pleasure lovers and entertainment experts, wrapped up in pleasing only themselves. In other words, they spent all their time thinking of ways to make life even more of an ongoing, everyday party centered on themselves.

The prophet Ezekiel said: "Now this was the sin of your sister Sodom: She and her daughters were arrogant, overfed and unconcerned; they did not help the poor and needy. They were haughty, and did detestable things before me. Therefore I did away with them as you have seen" (Ezekiel 16:49, 50).

Today most people wish they could win the lottery just once, even if they don't believe in buying tickets. Many people dream of what they'd do if they could have all the time and money in the world—even for a day. Yet money and free time, which seem like very good things, are what started the people of Sodom toward their terrible future fate. Because they lived useless, idle lives, they were easy targets for Satan's temptations. They embraced all the bad and hurtful things they could do to themselves and others. They became so evil that they blotted out the reflection of God—the beautiful image of God that He'd put in each of their lives. God's image should have shone through their characters, but it didn't. They became satanic rather than divine.

The story of Sodom is told as a warning to us today. Today's nifty electronic machines can do just about everything. You can sit all day and night in front of an electronic screen, moving only your fingers. So it's doubly important to know that idleness is one of the greatest curses of all. Too much free time makes your mind weak and twists your understanding about good things.

Like the evil warrior that he is, Satan is waiting to ambush people who let down their guard. He loves to take advantage of our free time to tempt us in some new, sneaky way. And he is at his satanic, most successful best when he comes to people during their idle hours.

That's how he won the hearts of the people of Sodom, for there was a whole lot of partying going on in that city. The streets and parks and houses were filled with people rocking with laughter, eating until they thought they'd burst, and drinking their hearts away. They didn't have TV, but all the vile, brutal, and cruel things that some people watch today they actually *did*. Just like the people who lived before the Flood and just like so many people today, people in Sodom loved to watch violent things. They also weren't afraid to curse God openly, and they stomped all over His law—His special and holy law.

The people living in Sodom had heard about the Flood from their grandparents and great-grandparents, for only a few hundred years had gone by since God had cleaned the world with water. They knew there was a limit to God's patience. They knew that His righteous anger had cut loose the rivers, opened the heavens, and sent torrents of water over the entire earth. But that didn't stop them from their wicked ways. They simply loved to be evil.

When Lot first moved to Sodom, it hadn't been that sinful. It was on its way to greater wickedness, to be sure, but rays of God's light still shone on the city, trying to save it from the moral darkness creeping across its streets.

The people living in Sodom knew about Abraham. They knew of his thoughtful life and his love for the unseen God. And they liked to make fun of him. In fact, quite a few "Abraham jokes" went around the city of Sodom. Of course, the people changed their tune a bit after Abraham had crashed in on their captors and saved them from a life of slavery.

Abraham and his men were brave warriors, but their little army had been greatly outnumbered. The armies of Chedorlaomer had been better armed, better trained, and much bigger than Abraham's. Everyone who had seen the victory of Abraham's army knew there had been a mighty hand involved in the battle—the hand of Abraham's God. "God must be with this man," they had whispered to one another.

The people of Sodom had also been amazed at Abraham's kind and unselfish ways. He acted so much differently from the way they did. They couldn't understand why he hadn't taken his share of the loot from the battle. In their hearts they knew that in Abraham they saw a better and brighter religion than any other they had ever seen. But still they did not give up their wicked ways.

Now Sodom's last night was drawing near. Dark clouds—the clouds of God's gathering anger—hovered over the city. Yet the people had shut out God's voice for so long that they had no idea that their hours of mercy were nearly over.

And so God sent His mighty angels flying through space, past Jupiter, Neptune, Mars, and thousands upon thousands of stars. Their destination was Planet Earth, and, more specifically, the city, the incredibly wicked city, of Sodom. They were on a mission, though not the kind of mission that God or His angels like to do. It was a mission of death and destruction.

CHAPTER 10

The Children Who Wouldn't

Whoosh! God's mighty angels zoomed in for a brilliant landing just a few miles from the gates of Sodom. No one saw them come, of course. And that's how they wanted it, for they wanted to walk into Sodom like two ordinary travelers. Perhaps it was one final test for the city. Having received a warm welcome by His servant Abraham, God wanted to see how His children in Sodom would treat His hidden heavenly messengers. For there was a battle going on in the city of Sodom—a battle between good and evil. On the side of good was Abraham's nephew Lot.

Lot had made a mistake in moving to

Sodom, and he knew it. But unfortunately for him, he was the only one in his family who seemed to recognize this fact. Lot's wife, a selfish and irreligious woman, loved the sights and sounds of the city. Lot's daughters had made friends in the city, and all but two had married local men. Perhaps a whole raft of grandchildren, in-laws, "outlaws," and other shirttail relations spent time with Lot. And he loved them, of course. Though he was turned off by the crude and ungodly conduct of the city's people—and even that of his family—in time he became almost used to it. But he still loved the true God. He was still a good man, and he tried to do what he could to help those in need.

One of Lot's special mission projects just so happened to be helping travelers who came to the city. Maybe he had learned the lesson of hospitality from his uncle Abraham, or maybe they both had learned it from Grandfather Terah. But wherever it came from, Lot's gracious way of treating tired travelers was a daily part of his life.

By this time the men of Sodom had sunk so low that they were always looking for new and more exciting forms of entertainment. If they'd had TV or video games, they would have loved to watch meanness and brutality. But since they had neither TV nor violent video games, they satisfied their appetite by stirring up trouble of their own. So the evil men of Sodom would watch for innocent travelers as they came through the gates of the city. Then, after they had a few beers in their bellies, they would gather as a mob and drag the visitors out of their houses. Some of their victims were killed, while others suffered torture and cruelty even worse than death.

Lot was aware of all this, of course. He couldn't stop it, for he was only one man. But as a man who loved God, Lot saved as many travelers as he could from the violent hands of his neighbors. Like the men of Sodom, Lot made it his mission to sit in the city gate. Like them, he was watching, watching for some tired person or family who made their way in. Then he would invite them to his home for dinner, give them a place to sleep, and protect them from the evil that stormed through the streets every night.

Standing by the city gate that evening, Lot saw God's mighty angels come in. Of course, they didn't look like angels to him. Just as Abraham had, he saw only tired travelers in need of water for their dry throats, warm food to eat, and a bed to sleep in.

Before the men of Sodom could make a move, Lot quickly stepped forward. "Would you like to stay at my home tonight?" he asked.

"No, thank you, we'll stay in the streets."

"Oh, please don't do that. The streets of this city aren't safe. Please come to my house and stay," Lot urged the visitors as the evil men scowled behind him.

"Very well," the angels replied. Soon they were seated in Lot's living room, enjoying a cool drink of water or perhaps even papaya juice while Lot's wife and two daughters fixed them dinner.

"What a beautiful home you have here," the angels must have said.

"Yes." Lot cleared his throat, looking around at the finely embroidered curtains, expensive dishes, and handcrafted artwork that decorated his large and elegant home. "There's quite a bit of money to be made in this city."

They were just finishing their evening meal when a thunderous knock rattled the front door.

"Excuse me, please," Lot said nervously. His heart sank as he slowly walked to the door. He knew who was there without even opening it. It was a mob of men, drunk and ready for action. Sick and tired of Lot's hospitality to strangers, they had decided to take matters into their own hands.

"Bring out your visitors, Lot!" they shouted viciously. "We want to get to *know* them!"

Bravely Lot stepped outside the door. He was taking his own life in his hands, and he knew it. But he had to save his guests.

"My brothers," he shouted above their roar. "Do not be so wicked!" But his words were like pouring oil on flames.

"Bring them out! Bring them out! Bring them out!" the mob chanted as their burly leader pushed to the front of the pack.

Lot met the drunken man with outstretched hands. "My brother, please don't bother these men," he pleaded, but the man just shoved Lot aside. Then Lot must have lost his mind for a moment, or perhaps he'd been so influenced by Sodom's vile culture that he didn't know what he was saying. But whatever his weak excuse, he actually offered his two daughters to those terrible men instead! One can only imagine the two young ladies trembling in fear behind their furious mother. Fortunately for the two girls, these wicked men didn't want them just then.

"Bring those guys out, Lot, or we'll take *you* in-

stead." The brawny bully lifted Lot by the lapels of his robe and slammed him against the door. Lot tried to break away, but there was no place to go. He tried to cry out for help, but he couldn't make a sound. The mindless, cursing mob packed even closer as the foul-breathed bully pounded on the door. The door trembled under his blows. Inside the house Lot's daughters screamed in terror.

Suddenly horror ripped through the crowd. Lot's attacker dropped him, and the vicious mob whimpered like a litter of lost puppies looking for their mother. In the same moment strong hands—kind hands, the same hands that had just struck the mob with blindness—grabbed Lot by his ripped robe and pulled him inside the door.

The angels didn't hide who they were any longer. "Listen, Lot, God has had it with this city!" Their voices shook with holy anger. "This place is so wicked that these people are missionaries of sin. God has sent us to destroy Sodom."

We can imagine Lot sinking into a chair, puzzled and frightened. Could he believe his ears?

"You must get out," the angels told him. "Save yourself and your family while there is still time. For when the sun comes up in the morning, fire will rain down from heaven. And this city—this beautiful but wicked city—will be no more."

We can only imagine the shock that Lot, his wife, and daughters felt at these words. Life as they knew it was over. They'd chosen to live in Sodom. They'd grown rich there and set down their roots. They had houses, land, and money in the bank, but their account in heaven was almost bankrupt. Time was running out.

They must get out or share in the city's doom.

Lot shook his head. Mrs. Lot was weeping. Their daughters clung to each other in fear. "What about my children and my grandchildren living inside the city?" he asked.

"Hurry! You must tell them now. There's not much time left."

So Lot hurried into the night, first to the home of one daughter, then the next. He didn't have to worry about the bloodthirsty mob anymore. They were still out in the street, but bouncing around like bumper cars in their blindness. Cursing and crying, they couldn't hurt him now.

Lot's first daughter and her husband were having a party. This was no surprise, of course. For in Sodom there were parties at just about every house every day of the week.

"You've got to leave the city!" Lot cried when his son-in-law opened the door. "Sodom is going to be destroyed at the break of day!"

"What's this? What are you talking about?" It was hard for Lot's son-in-law to shift from his merry mood and move into action. In fact, it was impossible. His guests had told so many jokes that night that this seemed like one more.

"Angels from heaven are here," Lot cried. "They told me to warn you that Sodom will be destroyed. We've got to leave right now."

"You've got to be kidding!" Lot's family laughed in his face. Perhaps he'd gone crazy. Or he was the biggest joker they'd ever seen. What foolishness! Fire from heaven!

"They won't come," Lot repeated over and over,

wringing his hands as he hurried back to his home. "Wife! Wife! They won't come."

Mrs. Lot wailed as she thought of her children and their babies and all of her special friends. "Nooooo," she cried. "No! I can't leave them."

"Yes, you must!" the angels urged. "If they won't come, then you must go without them."

But Lot seemed frozen, unable to move. He didn't think about how gracious it was for God to save him. He could only think of his children, the precious children he now had to leave behind.

Then God in His great mercy reached out of heaven and through the hands of His mighty angels took Lot, his wife, and their two daughters firmly by the hand and led them out of the city.

"Whatever you do, *don't look back,*" the angels told them as they hurried through the city gates. "Do you understand us? We are asking you not to look back, and you must obey!"

On and on they ran, panting for breath as the angels urged them to go even faster. Dust blew in their faces. Tears and dust blinded their eyes. But still the little family of four followed the angels toward the small city of Zoar.

And then a terrible thing happened. Lot's wife stopped. She turned, and she looked back toward the city of Sodom.

Lot and his daughters hardly knew that she had stopped. Their eyes were on the houses they saw just ahead, and they hurried to make it to its gate. *Boom!* As the morning light broke over the horizon a thunderous roar rolled across the heavens behind them. Then *kaboom, kaboom, kaboom!*

A hail of explosions pounded Lot's ears as God's "fighter pilots" bombed the cities of Sodom and Gomorrah with fire and brimstone. Above the thunderous booms rose shrieks and screams. A strange orange glow backlit the sky and reflected on the low hills surrounding Zoar.

I wish I had never gone to Sodom, Lot thought, fighting the urge to turn and look at the city he had chosen as his home. But he knew he must obey the angels, follow the voice that had told him that if he would save his own soul, he must never look back.

CHAPTER 11

Pillar of Fault

R emember Lot's wife."
These are some of the saddest words in the Bible. Lot's wife is not remembered because she was beautiful, which she probably was, or for the good things she undoubtedly did while she lived in Sodom. She is remembered for the most important action of her entire life. As she and her family fled from the doomed city of Sodom with the angels instructions in their ears, she paused, she turned, and she looked back—and was turned into a pillar of salt.

Unfortunately for Lot, there was plenty of blame to go around. Not only was there a pillar of salt in the story, but also there was a heaping "pillar of fault."

No doubt Lot spent much of the rest of his life saying to himself, "If only . . ." If only he had been a stronger leader. If only he had not moved near the gorgeous but extremely wicked cities of Sodom and Gomorrah. If only he had stayed near Abraham, where he could have benefited from the patriarch's godly example and good advice. If only he had pulled up stakes and left town right away when he had realized how the neighborhood children were influencing his own family for evil. If only his daughters hadn't married men of Sodom.

Perhaps Lot's wife could have learned from the godly example of Sarah. Instead, she had been led further and further from God by the pagan women of the plains. Worst of all, her huge mistake in turning back for one last look at Sodom was influenced by Lot himself.

Lot could have moved a whole lot faster when the angels told him to leave. But he didn't. He loved his children, and they had refused to leave. He was all torn up inside by love for his luxury home, his friends, and the wealth he had worked so hard to get. Add to that the outpouring of emotion by his wife, and Lot practically had to be dragged from the city of Sodom.

This whole story has so many lessons for us today. First, God is patient and kind, yet there will be a day of judgment.

People in the cities of Sodom and Gomorrah had sunk so far into the mud of sin that they had no desire to pull themselves out. They were pretty stubborn about it too. They had no intention of changing—not ever. Worse yet, by their defiance of

God and continual lives of sin, they were leading whole cities of people in the wrong direction. God had to do something about it.

Sometimes our loving God is faced with very hard choices. You see, if there is a rotten spot on your apple and you don't cut it out, it will ruin the whole apple.

The people of the world are God's children, the apple of His eye. But long ago there was a rotten spot called Sodom, and the rot (or the evil) was spreading so fast that a paring knife simply wouldn't stop it. So God had to throw out the bad apple.

This doesn't mean that God didn't love the people of Sodom and Gomorrah. His heart was broken by their stubborn ways. But time and time again when God knocked on the door of their hearts, they slammed it right in His face. They weren't happy simply to break God's rules—they stomped all over them. They were also involved in the export business, exporting their sinful lifestyle all over the then-known world. So God put a stop to it all, and that is called judgment.

But even on judgment day, our God is a God of mercy. Though the people of Sodom died in their sins, many other people were saved from their wicked influence. And it was a very special act of mercy when God saved the life of Lot.

The story of Lot, while one of the saddest in the Bible, should also be one of the most encouraging to Christians who are praying for friends and relatives who don't know Jesus.

Jesus Himself had told Abraham of His plan to destroy Sodom and Gomorrah. Abraham had been shocked, for his nephew Lot and his family lived there.

Abraham had asked—and even begged—God to

save Lot and his family. And God had been very patient with Lot. Although Lot was a good man himself, he had become pretty used to the wickedness all around him. So he had been shocked when two angels had brought the news that his home was about to be buried in brimstone.

But God had worked with Lot—even to the point of having His angels grab his hand to help him get moving when Sodom's last minutes were ticking down.

So whether you are praying for your mom, dad, grandparents, or someone else, do not give up hope. Pray with all your heart every day that God will send His angels to, if necessary, even take them by the hand and lead them into His love. God will never make anyone leave a life of sin, but you can be sure that in answer to your prayers, He will work mightily in the lives of people you love.

We should learn one more important lesson from the tragic story of Lot. It's about attitude—or should we say the need for an attitude adjustment. Despite all the mercy God showed to Lot, he didn't seem to appreciate it very much. Lot even asked God to spare one of the wicked smaller cities nearby so that he could move there. Even though God knew this was a bad idea, in His great kindness He did as Lot asked.

As God calls you away from a life of sin, you may feel very sad if your family doesn't follow Jesus as you do. But the happiness you feel by loving Jesus and being saved should be much greater than any sadness you feel over your family. If we stop to pity ourselves or play with sin, we may run into the same kind of trouble that Lot did. And if we love our families more than we love God, it will seem very hard to step out alone if they won't follow.

But if you step out firmly and follow Jesus in faith, there's a much better chance that your family will follow. So put your hand in the hand of Jesus. Give your life fully to Him. Never look back, and pray every day for your family.

You can be sure that God will send His angels to stand by their side, and, if they will only allow it, take them by the hand and draw them closer to Him. Some of your loved ones may never follow Jesus, but others will be encouraged because of your shining example. They will see you step out for Jesus, and before you know it, they'll be right by your side—with their backs to sin and their eyes on the heavenly kingdom.

CHAPTER 12

War of the Women

When compared to Lot and his family, Abraham and Sarah had a peaceful, happy life. They had money. They loved God. And because they ran their entire household by God's rules, they had a basically pleasant life together.

But an almost overwhelming sadness hung over their hearts. Abraham and Sarah badly wanted to have children. The Bible tells us that children are a blessing from the Lord, and both of these godly people longed for that blessing.

No doubt there were many children in Abraham's camp. But Abraham and Sarah wanted to hear the pitter-patter of little feet and the childish chatter of their own little one, and nothing else would do.

Having a child seemed especially important to them because God had promised that they would be the parents of a great nation. As you may remember, even Abraham's name promised that this prediction would be fulfilled. But as the years rolled by and no baby came, their hopes for having a child of their own became dimmer and dimmer.

Abraham and Sarah were human just like the rest of us. They wanted to trust God, but sometimes their faith was weak. So they kept trying to help God out by taking things into their own hands.

"I could adopt my servant Eliezer," Abraham had told God. But God had rejected that idea because He knew that He was going to give Abraham and Sarah their very own son. But when Sarah had a new idea, God didn't reject it. The reason He didn't say no was that Abraham and Sarah didn't ask His advice.

"Why don't you marry my maidservant?" Sarah asked Abraham. "You could have a baby by her, and it could be like our own."

The very idea must have seemed shocking at first. Abraham was happy with Sarah. He didn't want another wife. Yet the practice of men taking more than one wife had become very common in Abraham's day—so common, in fact, that people no longer thought of it as sin. If he had thought of this plan himself, Abraham might have worried about how Sarah would feel. But since she was the one who suggested it, he felt it would be all right.

So it was that Abraham married Sarah's servant, Hagar.

The Bible doesn't say how long Abraham's home remained happy after this marriage, but things probably fell apart right after the wedding. Sarah hadn't realized how jealous she would feel. As for Hagar, she started to feel a little uppity about her climb up the social ladder when she married Abraham.

Things got a whole lot worse when Hagar became pregnant with Abraham's child. Sarah was used to being treated with a great deal of respect by all of their servants, Hagar included. But Hagar got a new attitude when she found out she was going to give birth to a child that everyone believed would be the son promised by God, and her attitude wasn't a good one.

Soon Hagar was snipping and snapping at Sarah as if she were the queen of the house. And as you can only imagine, Sarah didn't like it one bit. Sarah felt bad enough that her servant was going to give birth to the child that she herself longed to have. To have Hagar lord it over her that she could have children and Sarah couldn't was just too much! Soon the tension between the two built up until Sarah said she couldn't take it anymore.

"Send her away!" she cried on Abraham's shoulder. "She makes my life miserable. She's not obedient anymore, and she mouths off to me. I know she's laughing with her friends because she's carrying your baby. I can't stand her any longer."

Abraham sighed. He loved Sarah very much, but he had come to love Hagar, too. After all, she was soon to have his baby. Although he felt distressed at the continual snipping and sniping, Abraham couldn't bear to send Hagar away. He decided to keep her around, but make peace by telling Sarah to deal with her maid as she wished. After all, Hagar was Sarah's handmaiden.

Sarah didn't need any encouragement. The Bible doesn't say exactly what Sarah did to Hagar, but it does tell us that the next time Hagar acted out of line Sarah mistreated her. Of course, Hagar wasn't about to let this happen. Though she had no money and no place to go, she did have two feet and she used them. Soon she was far away from Abraham and Sarah's camp, determined to put as much distance between her and Sarah as possible.

However, she couldn't hide from God.

"Hagar, Sarah's maid," an angel voice called out in the desert where Hagar was hiding. "Where did you come from, and where are you going?"

"I fled from my mistress, Sarah," Hagar replied.

"Go back to your mistress," the angel told her. "God wants you to be a good and humble worker."

This was hard medicine for Hagar to take, but God had words of encouragement for her too. Even though He was sending her back, God was sympathetic with Hagar.

"God has seen all the trouble you are having," the angel said. "He will bless the son you will have, and you will have many, many grandchildren." The angel also gave Hagar a comforting name for her son, the name of Ishmael, which means "God shall hear."

It could not have been easy for Hagar, but she went back to Sarah and worked as her servant. She must have said that she was sorry for her part in the trouble, and she must have tried to be more respectful. And it was a great moment for Hagar when Ishmael was born, for at once he was the darling of

Abraham's camp. And in spite of God's repeatedly telling Abraham that Sarah would be the mother of his promised son, Abraham didn't quite get it.

"O that Ishmael might be the one, the promised son, and live a good life before you," Abraham prayed to God.

Ishmael was the only son he had at this point, and Abraham loved him dearly. Hagar also wished with all her heart that Ishmael would be God's "son of the promise," and because of Abraham's own confusion on this point, the whole camp thought that Ishmael would be the one.

But God had made a promise, and He intended to keep that promise, even though it upset the plans of Ishmael, Hagar, and Abraham's whole encampment.

CHAPTER 13

Son of the Promise

Sometimes the longer you wait for something, the more special it seems when it comes. Perhaps at some point in your life you have been ravenously hungry, but the food just wasn't ready. You could smell that Thanksgiving roast baking in the kitchen, but you had to wait. A pumpkin pie would taste good to most people any day of the week, but it would be especially good to someone who was famished.

We don't know why God had Abraham and Sarah wait so long to have their baby. Perhaps He wanted them to learn patience. Perhaps He wanted the world around to take note that something important was going on, since even in those days 90-year-old women simply didn't have babies.

Whatever the reason, Abraham and Sarah waited a very long time. They waited so long that, even as people of faith, they had a pretty hard time truly believing it would happen.

When Jesus and the angels had visited Abraham on their way to destroy Sodom and Gomorrah, God Himself told Abraham that the promised baby would be coming soon. Sarah was sitting out of sight in her tent but listening to every word. And when she heard that, she couldn't quite stifle a chuckle.

I can't believe it! she thought to herself. Though she didn't laugh out loud, the Bible says that she "laughed within herself."

"Why is Sarah laughing?" God asked Abraham. "Is anything too hard for the Lord?"

Suddenly Sarah was afraid. Something told her that God was out there, and that she should have had more faith.

Sarah peered out of the tent. She hadn't meant to be disrespectful, but it just seemed too hard to believe. "I didn't laugh," she said.

God didn't spend time scolding or arguing with Sarah. "Yes, you did laugh," He simply said. Then the messengers were gone, leaving Abraham and Sarah—who were both close to the ripe old age of 100—to ponder on it all.

A year had come and gone since the heavenly visitors had eaten with Abraham that day. It had been an eventful year, for Sodom and Gomorrah had been destroyed. Lot's wife had turned into a pillar of salt. And as for Abraham and Sarah, they had been part of a painful and embarrassing situation with Abimelech, king of Gerar.

It seems that for being nearly 90 years old, Sarah was still very beautiful. She was so beautiful, in fact, that Abraham worried when he traveled that someone might kill him so they could have her. He was so worried that he made the same mistake he had made before.

You remember that Sarah was Abraham's half-sister, as well as his wife, so Abraham told her to say that she was his sister. Again, this showed that Abraham still struggled to have faith in God. Instead of letting God lead, he kept taking matters into his own hands.

Abimelech did notice Sarah. More than that, he moved her right into his palace. How amazing! Just when God was about to give Abraham and Sarah the long-awaited baby, they put themselves in a situation in which Sarah very nearly became the wife of a heathen king.

But God stepped in again.

"Hello, Abimelech," a voice boomed out in the night, speaking to the king through a dream. "You might as well be a dead man."

"What! What have I done?" he cried out.

As far as he knew, he had been doing right. And though Abimelech was worshipping pagan gods, he knew God's voice when he heard it in a dream.

"You have taken another man's wife, intending to make her your wife."

"But I didn't know anything about it, Lord. They both said that she was his sister."

"I know, Abimelech," God reassured him. "That's

why the punishment I have given you so far can be undone. But you had better take care of it right away, and I mean what I say."

"Yes, Lord!"

When Abimelech woke up he was not only shocked but angry. Even though he was a pagan, he did not want to commit the sin of adultery. Fortunately, and in the providence of God, he had not touched Sarah.

Abimelech ordered Abraham to come before him. "What have you done?" he demanded.

Abraham tried to explain, but it was a lame excuse. "If it was anyone else, and if your God didn't watch over you so closely," the king said, "you and I would be fighting a war."

Abimelech soundly scolded the couple, gave them some gifts, and sent them on their way. He told them they could live in his country wherever they pleased.

The very next chapter of the Bible tells us that "the Lord was gracious to Sarah as he had said, and the Lord did for Sarah what he had promised. Sarah became pregnant and bore a son to Abraham in his old age, at the very time God had promised him" (Genesis 21:1, 2).

What joy there must have been in Sarah's tent that day! How happy she and Abraham were to have their own baby after waiting so long. For Sarah was 90 years old when Isaac was born, and Abraham was 100.

"God has brought me laughter, and everyone who hears about this will laugh with me," Sarah said (verse 6).

Yes, it is quite amazing and even funny that a 90-

year-old woman would have a baby. Today many 90-year-olds are in a nursing home if they are around at all. If they are especially spry, they may still drive a car or work in their garden. But have a baby? Ridiculous!

If she's not listed there already, Sarah should be in the *Guinness Book of World Records*. But really, she couldn't quite take the credit. It was God who "did for Sarah what he had promised." What a wonderful reminder that, even if it takes 20, 90, or 1,000 years, God really does keep His promises.

CHAPTER 14

Unhappy Wife, Unhappy Life

The birth of Baby Isaac, which brought so much joy to the hearts of Abraham and Sarah, was seen in quite a different light by Hagar and Ishmael. It was the death knell for Hagar's fondest hope that Ishmael was the son God had promised, the one to inherit the riches of Abraham at his death.

Years before, Hagar had obeyed the angel's command to come back and be Sarah's servant. Her heart was still bitter, however, over the years of tension between herself and her mistress. Now Ishmael was 13 years old. He was old enough to understand what was going on and to be very angry too. When

Baby Isaac was born, Ishmael got knocked off the pedestal that everyone but Sarah had placed him on. For 13 years he had been the favored one—the only son. He had been led to believe that he was the "son of promise," the one through whom all families of the world would be blessed. Now this pudgy little upstart had come and taken his spot. Hagar didn't take this too kindly, and neither did Ishmael.

Things really started to spiral out of control the day Sarah caught Ishmael making fun of little Isaac. This was probably the last straw in a long string of problems.

"Abraham, you must send them away!" Sarah said through clenched teeth. She may have mentioned the idea before, but this time she was not only persistent but insistent. "There will be nothing but trouble as long as they stay."

Abraham sighed. Over the years there had been plenty of squabbles between Sarah and Hagar, and he was always stuck in between. Abraham loved Ishmael. He also loved Hagar. But he had been married to Sarah for decades before Hagar was even born. She was his first wife and in the eyes of God *the* wife.

The very idea of sending Hagar and Ishmael away made Abraham sick to his stomach. He knew things couldn't go on as they were, but he didn't want to hurt Ishmael or Hagar. Then God, who is always ready to help us when we are confused, sent his angel to give Abraham words of advice.

"Listen to Sarah," the angel said. "Your home will never be happy again, the way things are." Then God promised Abraham that He would be with Ishmael. He promised that He would keep Ishmael safe and make him a great nation also.

Abraham knew what he must do. Sarah was right. There was no way to restore peace to their home without hurting somebody—and hurting them badly. But peace must be restored; otherwise their home would never be happy again. And so with a heavy heart Abraham called Hagar and Ishmael to his tent.

"I love you, Ishmael," he must have said as he put his arm around his firstborn son. "This is the hardest thing I have ever had to do."

Then he turned to Hagar.

"I am so sorry," he whispered, handing some supplies to Hagar and hugging her one last time. "But you must go."

The Bible doesn't tell us how Ishmael and Hagar reacted. One can only guess that they were shocked, horrified, and scared stiff all in one terrible moment. This made Abraham feel even worse, yet once he had made his decision he knew he could not back down.

Perhaps Ishmael promised to stop making fun of Isaac, or Hagar said she would try to do better. Whatever the case, and whatever their pleadings, Abraham knew it would never work. As hard as it was to send them out into the desert, God had promised him that He would take care of them. He also knew that if they didn't go, his home would always be filled with sniping and tension.

God wanted Abraham to have a happy life—and a happy wife. This could never happen with a second wife and her son competing for attention in the home. The angel had made things clear. As painful as it was, Abraham learned the hard way that in marriage, three really is a crowd.

CHAPTER 15

The Ultimate Sacrifice

Throughout his life Abraham had a very special relationship with God. In fact, the Bible calls Abraham the friend of God. This doesn't mean that Abraham was any closer to God than any of us can be today. God loves each person in the world just as much as he loved Abraham. But because Abraham had responded deeply to God's love and spent many hours with Him, he had grown very close to God.

Unfortunately, Abraham had also let God down several times in his life. Even though God had made him some very special promises, time and again Abraham tried to take things into his own hands. And

when we take things into our own hands, this means we don't trust God enough to let Him take care of a situation for us.

When Abraham married Hagar instead of waiting for God to give Sarah a baby, he was not trusting God as he should. When Abraham twisted the truth and told people that Sarah was his sister when really she was his wife, he was mistrusting God once again. Sadly, Abraham told this lie not once, but twice in his life.

Now, God has very specific ways of helping us learn to do right. One of the things God does when we make wrong decisions that make a mess of lives is to allow the same temptations to come again. Often God gives us the same test over and over until we get it right. In the case of Abraham, God replaced those earlier, easier tests about trust and faith with one of the biggest tests anyone has ever had to face. This test involved the "son of the promise," Isaac.

As the years passed, Isaac grew from a tiny baby to a toddler, a toddler to a boy, a boy into a teenager, and a teenager into a wonderful young man. After all those years of waiting for their promised son, you can be sure that Isaac was the apple of Abraham and Sarah's eyes and the light of their lives. They loved being his parents and did their best to raise him to love and honor God.

They must have done a good job too, because the Bible never gives us any indication that Isaac was a spoiled brat or anything like that. Instead, as you will soon see, he was a very courteous and obedient boy.

Late one night when Abraham was sound asleep, an angel came with a strange command. He told Abraham to take his son, his only son Isaac, and, of all things, offer him up as a sacrifice to God! This command went against everything Abraham had ever dreamed of. Heathen people all around him offered their children as sacrifices to idols, but worshippers of God never did.

"Why would God ask me to do something that goes against His rules?" Abraham must have wondered. "How can Isaac be the son of the promise—and have many children—if he's dead?"

It seemed unlikelier than ever that God would send another son by Sarah, as she was probably more than 100 years old by then. But the Bible doesn't say that Abraham argued with God. It says only that Abraham did as God asked.

Abraham had spent so much time with God, and knew God so well, that he recognized the voice he had heard as God's voice, even if it had told him to do a strange and terrible thing. And at last, Abraham, who had not always trusted God as much as he should have, was willing to trust God with his son's life. He trusted God enough to believe that if Isaac should lose his life, God would either bring him back to life or send another son. He trusted God enough to know that, if God asked him to do something extraordinary or even very strange, there must be a very good reason.

So Abraham rolled off his mat and stood up. He put on his daytime clothes, then crept to where Isaac lay.

"Isaac," he called quietly. The young man stirred as he heard someone call his name.

"Isaac," Abraham hissed in a whisper. "Wake up!"

"Yes, Father?"

"Get up quickly, son. We're going up to the mountain of God to offer a sacrifice."

The last thing Abraham wanted or needed was for Sarah to know about God's command. This was between him and God, and no matter how much it hurt, he intended to do what God had asked.

So Isaac stumbled out of his bed, and quickly they went on their way.

Some youngsters think their parents are cruel if they awaken them before noon. And kids whose parents wake them up early and make them do chores may think their mom and dad are especially cruel. But what about a mom or dad who'd wake up their child to do the terrible thing God had asked Abraham to do?

Insane, you might say. Bizarre. Cruel. Extremely strange. If there had been a social service department in those days, somebody would have called it. But Isaac had only one caseworker, and His name was God.

And so father and son headed out into the darkness. Two servants and a donkey bearing a load of firewood went with them. Abraham, whose every thought was of God's unusual command, was strangely silent. And Isaac, still rubbing the sleep out of his eyes, was probably too tired to care. So they trudged on together, closer and closer to a mountain where there would be death.

CHAPTER 16

God Will Provide

It was a three-day trip to the mountain of sacrifice, and the nearer they got to the place, the more solemn and quiet Abraham grew. Perhaps Isaac noticed that he was in a very sober mood, and chose to be quiet too. But at some point, as the sun peeked over the nearby mountains, Isaac noticed a problem.

He had watched his father offer sacrifices many times before. He knew all about building an altar, and the fire, and the sacrifice on the altar. But now his father told the servants, "Stay here with the donkey while I and the boy go over there. We will worship, and then we will come back to you" (Genesis 22:5).

The Bible tells us that "Abraham took the wood for the burnt offering and put it on his son Isaac, and he himself carried the fire and the knife" (verse 6). Then, as they hiked up the mountain together, Isaac noticed that something very important was missing.

"My father," he said, "the wood and the fire are here, but where is the lamb for the burnt offering?"

Abraham's heart was already breaking. The thought of giving up his son—the one he loved so much and had waited for so long—was a grief greater than he thought he could bear. But somehow in his tender fatherly love he wanted to shield his son from the bitter truth as long as he could. Let Isaac whistle as he walked up the mountain. Let him enjoy the singing of the birds, the clear morning air, and the beauty of yet one more sunrise. For after today Isaac's life would be over.

Somehow in the middle of his grief Abraham managed to give Isaac a calm but reassuring answer. "My son, God will provide Himself a sacrifice."

These words seemed to satisfy Isaac, who asked nothing more about it. Together they trudged to the top of a hill to one of Abraham's altars. Together they repaired the altar and placed the wood upon it. Then Abraham could keep silent no more. The moment of truth had come.

Putting his hands on Isaac's shoulders, he told him of God's command.

"You mean I am going to die today?" Isaac was shocked and terrified. We can imagine that it took him a few minutes to comprehend fully what his father had said. Yet he was so trusting and had such complete faith in both God and his father that he willingly did as God asked.

Isaac was many years younger than Abraham and surely a lot stronger. He could have turned and fled down the mountain. He could have argued or struggled or fought. But Isaac did none of those things. The Bible doesn't record what Isaac said to Abraham right at that moment. Perhaps it was a boy's version of the words that Mary, the mother of Jesus, would say so many years later when told she would have a son: "I am the Lord's servant. May it be to me as you have said" (Mark 1:38).

In other words, Isaac was not only obedient but willing to be obedient. What a wonderful young man he was! He had his whole life ahead of him. As Abraham's heir he could be rich and happy with many children and grandchildren. Yet he was willing to give it all up if that was what God had called him to do.

Many young people don't like to sacrifice or to give up anything that they like. Even if there's a very good reason to give up something they like, they don't want to do it. How different this was from Isaac. The only reason given for giving up his life was that God had called him to do so. The idea of a human sacrifice was totally opposite to everything he knew about the great and living God. Never in his wildest dreams would he have thought God would call him to do this. But God had called, and he would obey.

The next few moments saw one of the saddest goodbyes in the Bible. Abraham must have told Isaac how much he loved him and that somehow—though he didn't know how—God would work all this out. As he held Isaac close, the tears streamed down his

beard onto the broad young shoulders of his son. He must have hugged him and hugged him—but not for too long, because Abraham knew he had to let go. He could not linger at God's command as Lot had. And so Isaac climbed up onto the altar. And Abraham—the same Abraham who hated the fighting and blood in the battle of the kings and who hated war and killing—raised a knife overhead, determined to drive it into the heart of his son.

With his left hand on Isaac's shoulder, Abraham closed his eyes and with all his might started to bring the knife down. Suddenly an unseen hand stopped his arm midair. The knife clattered out of his hand, and he fell over the altar, exhausted with the emotion and stress of it all, yet determined to do as God had asked.

"Abraham!" A voice echoed over the mountain. "What are you doing?"

"Just as You said, Lord," Abraham mumbled, still trembling from the mental trauma of trying to kill his own son.

"Now I know that you love Me," God told him, "because you have not withheld from me your son, your only son" (Genesis 22:12).

So the truth came out that this had all been a test.

The trip to the mountaintop altar had taken three days—three days of agony for Abraham. He had had plenty of time to rationalize, plenty of time to doubt, plenty of time to wonder what he would say to Sarah. But he had held firm. He knew what God had asked, and determined to do it.

The example of Abraham and Isaac stands like a pillar of light today. There are many who think that faith—or believing—is all it takes to follow God. But some types of faith don't mean a thing. The Bible says that "the devils also believe, and tremble." That was not the type of faith that Abraham and Isaac had. They had what is called a "saving faith"— a faith so strong that it had to result in action. Because they truly believed God, they were willing to do what He asked. In the words of the apostle John, "This is love for God: to obey his commands" (1 John 5:3).

Things go on that we cannot see. The Bible tells us that when the angels of God gathered to discuss what was happening in the universe, Satan sometimes showed up at their meetings. In these meetings Satan loved to point out when God's people failed some test.

"Look at Your good friend Abraham," Satan jeered at God. "The father of many nations is the master of little white lies. He tells people his wife is his sister, just to save his skin. What a bad example he was to Abimelech and Pharaoh. Why, You had to step in to save his neck!"

The good angels shook their heads in frustration and started to plug their ears, but Satan was surly and just warming up.

"Then there's this little matter of the second wife, Hagar. Hello? Isn't this against Your rules? She brings out the worst in Sarah—and whatever happened to the happy little home?"

But things changed after Abraham's big test. The next time Satan showed up in the heavenly council meetings, the good angels had a message for him.

"Did you see the huge test that Abraham, friend of God, just passed? Did you see the faith and obedience of Isaac, his son? Does this not show, once and for all, that for all the mistakes he's made, Abraham truly is the friend and servant of God?"

The good angels, who were thrilled to see such a wonderful victory, couldn't wipe the angelic smiles off their faces. And Satan stomped off in a huff. Meanwhile, kazillions of miles away, far down on Planet Earth, "Abraham believed God, and it was credited to him for righteousness,' and he was called God's friend" (James 2:23).

CHAPTER 17

Search for a Soul Mate

Abraham was an old man now. Throughout his life he had been pretty good at learning from not only his own mistakes, but also the mistakes of others. From his own mistake in bringing Hagar in as a second wife, Abraham knew how much sadness an unhappy marriage can bring. Hagar was an Egyptian, familiar with the gods that they worshipped. She had not known and loved the God of heaven the way Abraham and Sarah did, and this had made things even harder. There was a constant tug-of-war between right and godless living, and Ishmael was in the middle of it. In his old age Ishmael came back to the faith of his father. But there were many years of godless, bitter living before that happened.

Abraham watched the unhappy life of Ishmael with sadness. He watched how first Hagar, then Ishmael's heathen wives, led his son further and further away from God. Abraham was also very well aware of how Lot's wife had influenced her husband to move further and further from his uncle's faith.

In spite of the many childless years and the mistakes they had made, Abraham's marriage to Sarah had been basically happy. Sarah loved God, and had been a wonderful wife. She had passed to her rest now and was sleeping peacefully in the grave, awaiting the resurrection. But Abraham had not forgotten how important Sarah and her love for God had been in making theirs a happy home. And he wanted the same type of home—and wife—for Isaac.

There was just one problem. No young women lived nearby who wholeheartedly loved and worshipped the God of heaven. It was the custom for parents to choose a wife or husband for their sons and daughters, and Abraham had been looking. But he just couldn't find anyone suited to be Isaac's wife.

No doubt Abraham had a little "laundry list" of qualities he was looking for. It would be great if the young woman were pretty, for Sarah had been very beautiful. But Abraham was looking much deeper than that. He wanted someone who was courteous, gracious, faithful, and energetic. But most of all, he wanted Isaac to marry a girl who truly loved God.

At some point Abraham realized that his best chance to find a young woman who loved the God of heaven would be among his own relatives back in Mesopotamia. This was a problem, because it was a very long way to Mesopotamia. The trip would be made by camels and would take a long time.

Perhaps Abraham was getting too old to make a trip, or maybe he didn't feel like traveling. Whatever the case, he called on one of his faithful servants—one who had been his right-hand man for many years—to help with this important task.

A lot of trust was involved in this whole wife-finding operation. Isaac trusted Abraham to choose the right woman for him. Abraham trusted Eliezer to find the right bride, and all three of the men put their trust in God.

The story of Isaac and his soon-to-be bride is one of the most beautiful love stories in the Bible, and we can learn important things from it. First, notice how much care Abraham took to find the right wife for Isaac. He didn't just go down the street and say that anyone would do.

Because Isaac would inherit the promises of God to Abraham, he too would be the father of many nations. This made the choosing of Isaac's wife all the more important. She needed to be somebody who would help lead Isaac closer to—rather than further away from—God. This was made even more important by the fact that Isaac had a very tender and loving personality. Abraham knew that Isaac was a quiet man who would be greatly influenced by his wife. This was not bad, for not everyone is a leader. But it made choosing just the right girl more important than ever.

Some young people may feel that whom they marry isn't quite so important, since they don't have the same calling as did Abraham or Isaac. Chances are that you personally don't feel called to be the father—or mother—of many nations. But the examples given us in the Bible show over and over that whom you marry is very important.

If you have questions about that, think of the examples of Samson and Solomon, whose ungodly wives led them far from the God they had once loved. The Bible says, "Do not be yoked together with unbelievers" (2 Corinthians 6:14). The King James Version puts it this way: "Be ye not unequally yoked." In other words, if you are a Christian, do not marry someone who doesn't love and obey Jesus.

In Bible times two oxen were yoked, or hitched, together to pull a plow. In order to do the best job plowing, the animals pulling together needed to be the same type and size. You wouldn't hitch up a poodle with an ox, or an ox with an elephant, and expect them to go anywhere. They would naturally pull in different directions.

The same thing is true when two people get "hitched." If the home is going to be godly, the couple must pull together. The Bible does say that if a Christian and non-Christian are already "hitched," they should not get "unhitched." The Christian should love and pray for the non-Christian partner, for the partner may come to love and serve Jesus too. But it is unwise to marry someone who believes differently from you. Most married couples have enough differences without adding a very wide gap in what each one believes about God.

No doubt these thoughts were very much on Abraham's mind as he sent his trusted servant off on a journey that—in addition to being very important—

was expensive and dangerous. But it would all be worthwhile if the right girl could be found for his beloved son Isaac.

CHAPTER 18

Man at the Well

The day probably started just like any other for the young woman named Rebekah. Life wasn't exactly fast-paced in those days, you know. Perhaps she and her family had morning worship, followed by breakfast, then a dividing out of the daily chores. Rebekah already knew one of her main jobs for the day—watering her father's flocks.

This was no small job, as camels especially drink a lot of water!

It seems that many small towns have some sort of hub or meeting place where people bump shoulders and chat about the weather or other happenings in their world. Today it might be the town square, the post office, or a grocery store, but in Rebekah's time it was the town well—at least for the young ladies who lived nearby.

Everyone had to get water, and they got it with leather buckets, rope, and a crank. The weather got pretty hot in Mesopotamia, the cattle and camels could be thirsty, and, all in all, the whole process sounds a whole lot like something called *work*.

However, this didn't stop Rebekah from being cheerful about her task. From a young age she had developed a willing, helpful, and courteous spirit. Imagine if Rebekah had been in a grumpy mood when Eliezer and his 10 camels showed up at the well. Imagine if she had been snippy by nature or had taken pleasure in hurling insults at other girls—and if Eliezer had seen this. Of course, if she had been like that, she wouldn't have been a good wife for Isaac, so Eliezer would not have chosen her anyway. Still, how important it is always to be on our best behavior, since we live in God's presence every day of our lives.

The Bible says, "Be not forgetful to entertain strangers: for thereby some have entertained angels unaware" (Hebrew 13:2). In the case of Rebekah, she did not entertain a stranger, but she was being watched—and chosen—by a stranger, her future husband's servant.

Eliezer had a few things going for him in this errand. He understood the importance of his mission, and he trusted God to guide him. Back home, Abraham and Isaac were praying that God would lead Eliezer to just the right girl, and during the long, slow days of travel Eliezer had a lot of time to talk to God about it as well. He did not want to let his master down or make a mistake on such an important matter. So he asked God to guide him and even asked for a sign.

Now, Eliezer was a wise and careful man. He knew that the village well would be a pretty good place for a man to look for a wife, even if the wife was for someone else. Here it was possible to see most of the young ladies of the area, and working no less! He could see what they looked like, how they interacted with one another, and how graceful and energetic they might be.

Eliezer decided to keep quiet about who he was and why he was there until God had made things clear to him. If he'd announced that he'd come from Canaan to find a wife for a rich man's son, girls might have lined up to campaign for the job, and he didn't want that. This whole thing must be left in God's hands.

And God, who cares as deeply for you and me today as He did for Abraham, Isaac, and Eliezer, didn't let His servant down. Indeed, He made things abundantly clear.

It started when one young woman stood out from the crowd. Apparently God didn't want Eliezer to come home with the wrong girl anymore than Abraham or Isaac did. Eliezer watched closely as Rebekah filled her pitcher with water and balanced it on her shoulder. As she stepped away from the well he walked over to her.

"May I have a drink of water?" he asked.

"Most certainly you may," she replied. Her gracious smile melted even an older gentleman like Eliezer right in his tracks. "And I will draw water for your camels, also."

Then Rebekah went right to work, cheerfully pulling up bucket after bucket of water until the large water trough was filled and every last hump on every last camel was satisfied.

It wasn't until then that Eliezer asked Rebekah her name. Imagine his joy and thankfulness when he discovered that this beautiful girl who seemed so perfectly suited for Isaac not only worshipped the true God, but was part of Abraham's extended family.

Stepping over to one of his camels, Eliezer pulled out some beautiful and expensive gifts for Rebekah. He then told her who he was, and asked whether he might stay at her father's house. While he waited at the well, she hurried home to tell her family about the stranger who'd turned out to be the servant of a relative. Then Rebekah's brother Laban ran back to the well to invite Eliezer to his home.

A lot of hospitality was extended to visitors in those days. So Laban and Rebekah's family put together a nice meal as quickly as they could, and invited Eliezer to join them for supper.

"I cannot eat until I have told what my errand is" was Eliezer's reply. He was so excited about how God had led him to Rebekah that he could not wait to share it. More than that, he was eager to hear the family's—and particularly Rebekah's—response to the reason for his trip. He also felt that no matter how hungry he was, finding a wife for Isaac was much more important than food. He may have wanted Rebekah's family to understand that too.

Now it was the turn for Rebekah's family—and the young lady herself—to be surprised. What had started as a regular, ordinary day was suddenly extraordinary. To the family's credit, they handled the sudden marriage proposal quite well. They loved Rebekah dearly and no doubt didn't want to see her go. They knew that they'd never see her again. Yet they trusted God more and clearly saw His leading in the whole situation.

No doubt there were many water wells in Mesopotamia in those days with many young ladies drawing water from those wells. But God led Abraham's servant to the right well and to the right young lady at the right time. Laban's family was willing to accept that by faith, so they gave their permission for Rebekah to go with Eliezer.

It's thought that women didn't have much freedom during Bible times, and in many cases this was true. But in the beautiful story of Rebekah—which God gave as an example of how things should be—Rebekah did have a choice. Her family was wise enough to understand that if she didn't want to go, her marriage wouldn't be happy. So they called Rebekah and asked an important question: "Will you go with this man?"

Here is where we learn some other important things about Rebekah. She could have gone because it sounded like a great adventure. She could have gone because she wanted to get away from her family or because she wanted to marry a very rich man. But none of those is the reason that Rebekah said yes.

Rebekah said yes because she had faith in God and believed He was leading in her life. And she trusted God enough to know that somewhere many miles away was a loving soon-to-be husband who would make her very happy. Now, that's faith! It must have made God and the angels smile to see Rebekah trust God so fully. Less than 24 hours after meeting a stranger at the village well Rebekah was on a camel on her way to a new life, new home, and the man of her dreams. What an experience! When it comes to fascinating stories, the Bible beats the best novel that was ever written. Truth is not only stranger than fiction—it's better than fiction.

CHAPTER 19

A Match Made
in Canaan

It was hundreds of miles from Rebekah's home to where Abraham and Isaac lived. There were mountains and rivers to cross, and a scorching desert that Eliezer and the caravan most likely went around. They may have faced danger on the trip, and they certainly saw all different kinds of scenery.

No doubt the bride-to-be had plenty of time to think, plan, and pray as she traveled. And far, far away in the land of Canaan, Isaac was praying too. In fact, he often went into the fields to meditate—which means to think—and pray. This was not the type of meditation that some people do today, for which they empty their minds completely. No, Isaac was filling his mind with prayer, deep thoughts about God, and plans for his upcoming marriage.

There were no cell phones or text messages in those days, so Isaac had no real idea of exactly when Eliezer and the caravan would arrive. He also might have wondered, at least once, whether any young lady from his father's house would be willing to make such a trip when she could stay and be close to her family.

Then one day while walking out in the field Isaac saw a caravan at the edge of the horizon. He stopped and watched. After a while the camels grew closer and closer until at last he recognized his father's servants. Meanwhile Rebekah, who no doubt had been told they were nearing her new home, climbed down from her camel and put on a veil to meet the man she would marry.

The Bible is silent about many of the details of this story. Was it love at first sight? Did Isaac and Rebekah get married right away? What went through their minds when they first saw each other? The Bible doesn't say, but leaves plenty of room for us to imagine what happened.

However, the Bible is very clear about the end result. "Isaac brought her into the tent of his mother Sarah, and he married Rebekah. So she became his wife, and he loved her; and Isaac was comforted after his mother's death" (Genesis 24:67).

What a tender picture of a very happy start in life for this newlywed couple! And what an upside-down way of choosing a mate compared to how it is done today.

Many young people do not want their parents' advice in choosing a husband or wife. They don't care what their parents think about it. Some even feel that the person they marry is none of their parents' business.

But God gave us parents for a reason. They have been around the block a few times, so to speak, and have seen many things that we haven't. Because of this, parents may see red flags or warning signs about the potential mate that young people in love can miss.

If there was ever a time to ask for advice, it is before getting married. Whom you choose for your husband or wife will affect your future happiness for years and years to come. In making such an important decision, it pays to be careful. If your own parents are not available or would not give godly advice, ask the counsel of someone you trust. And by all means, talk to God about it a lot.

Isaac was a very patient man. He did not run out and find his own wife, but followed the custom of the day in waiting for Abraham to help him. Isaac trusted both his earthly father and his heavenly Father to make one of the most important decisions of his life, with no questions asked. And Isaac was rewarded for his faith with a happy marriage to a very gracious, courteous, helpful, and beautiful wife. He couldn't have done it better if he had ridden a camel all the way to the city of Haran, where Rebekah's family lived, and picked her out himself.

What a beautiful story this is, ending with the words "he loved her." It seems safe to say that she loved him too, very much.

FAMILY BIBLE STORY
SERIES

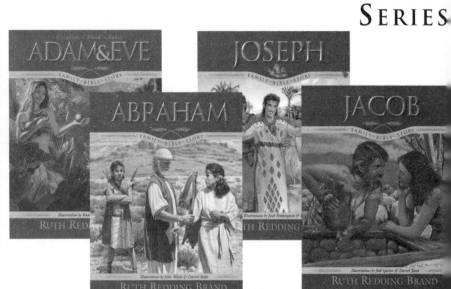

One of the most extensively researched Bible story books on the market today, this series offers features which give background information to engage every member of the family, young and old alike. Written by Ruth Redding Brand and illustrated by distinguished artists, these carefully researched and beautifully illustrated books will make Bible characters come alive for your children. Every name, place, and custom is carefully explained. Hardcover. Available individually or as a set.

Abraham, 109 pages. ISBN 0-8280-1856-1
Adam & Eve, 95 pages. ISBN 0-8280-1850-2
Jacob, 127 pages. ISBN 0-8280-1852-9
Joseph, 87 pages. ISBN 0-8280-1854-5

Quick order online at www.AdventistBookCenter.com
Call 1-800-765-6955
Visit your local Adventist Book Center®
Or ask for it wherever books are sold

REVIEW AND HERALD®
PUBLISHING ASSOCIATION